Learn to Crochet Socks the
Toe-Up Way! ™

D1560708

General Information

Many of the products used in this pattern book can be purchased from local craft, fabric and variety stores, or from the Annie's Attic Needlecraft Catalog (see Customer Service information on page 16).

Introduction

HOW TO CUSTOM FIT A BASIC CROCHETED TOE-UP SOCK WITH AN AFTER-THOUGHT HEEL

If this is your first time crocheting a sock, try using some nice, inexpensive worsted weight yarn. With thicker yarn, an average crocheter can complete at least one sock in 6 hours or less. Worsted weight yarn makes great slippers for around the house or sleeping. Start with 2 or more 50-gram balls and a hook at least 2 sizes smaller than the manufacturer's recommendation.

Working in a tight tension will improve the durability of your socks.

HERE ARE USEFUL TERMS:

Ankle–The joint where the foot meets the calf of the leg.

Arch–The curve on the bottom of the foot.

Ball of the foot–The area on the bottom of the foot between the toes and the arch.

Calf–The lower portion of the leg between the ankle and the knee.

Heel–The back part of the foot below and behind the ankle.

Instep–The top of the foot between the toes and the ankle.

The next step is the often-dreaded tension swatch. Make the swatch in single crochets at least 5 inches square. In general, a bigger swatch will yield more accurate gauge measurements.

To measure the gauge, weave darning needles through the swatch 4 inches apart, but not too close to any of the edges.

A straight-edge ruler will yield a more accurate measurement than a tape measure. Set the ruler aside and count the single crochets in 1 row between the needles. Below is a work sheet to note your results:

1. With measuring tape, measure the circumference around the widest part of the instep of the foot (*variable B*). You may have

thought you would never use the algebra they made you learn in high school but, yes, you do need to use math when you crochet. A toe-up sock is just that—the work starts at the toe. Generally, adult socks start with a chain 2 inches long, or 1 inch long for a child's sock.

2. Take the number of stitches in 4 inches (*variable A*) and divide that number by 2 for adults and 4 for children, add 1 for the turning chain $(A/2+1)$.

3. Begin shaping the toe by working into both sides of the chain with 3 single crochets in the last stitch on each end of the chain, excluding the turning chain.

4. When the first round is complete, the number of single crochets should be twice the number of starting chains. Some sock patterns will give you stitch counts for each round of the toe.

5. Place a stitch marker in the center stitch on each end of the chain. Increase in the stitch before and after each marker.

6. Increase until there are enough stitches to go around the instep.

7. **More algebra:** Take the number of stitches in 4 inches (*A in step 2*), divide that number by 4 to get the number of stitches per inch $(A/4)$. Multiply that number by the number of inches around the thickest part of the foot $(A/4 \times B)$ to get the number of stitches needed (*variable C*).

8. If you want to know the number of rows you will need, take the number of stitches for the circumference of the foot (C), subtract the number of stitches in 4 inches (A) and add 2. Divide that number by 4 to get the number of rows of increases $[(C-A+2)/4]$.

9. Work the instep even to the ankle. If there is a significant difference between the circumference at the ball of the foot and the largest part of the foot, the sock will be a little baggy just above the toe. You may want to modify the pattern.

10. Measure the circumference at the ball of the foot *(variable D)*. Subtract D from B *(B-D)* and multiply the new number by the number of stitches per inch *[(B-D) x A/4]*. This is the number of stitches you will need to increase between the toe and the ankle. Work the instep until it touches the front of the ankle or about 2 inches shorter than the length of the foot.

11. Work the instep even and be creative in the stitch combinations.

12. Crocheted fabric will bias when worked in continuous rounds. To prevent the bias, turn work at the end of each round. Work one round from the right side and the next from the wrong side.

13. An after-thought heel is worked last, after the ankle and cuff. Generally, the circumference of the largest part of the foot is about the same as the circumference of the ankle. To make a space for the heel, make a chain and skip half of the stitches around the instep.

14. Chain stitches do not stretch the same as other stitches. Use a slightly larger hook to make the chain or add a couple extra stitches to help the sock fit comfortably. Foundation stitches stretch very nicely. In a foundation stitch, you work the chain with each stitch.

15. Work a few rows of the ankle before trying on the sock. If the chain feels tight around the back of the heel, rip back to the instep and add a few more rows. If the toe is baggy, remove a few rows from the instep.

16. The ankle and the cuff are the place to let your creativity shine. You can work in continuous rounds or back and forth, joining with a slip stitch at the end of each round.

17. Crochet is not as resilient as knitting. For a higher cuff, work some elastic into the ribbing to help hold up the sock. Increase as necessary to fit over the calf.

18. Start the toe with the inside end of the yarn. Work part of the ankle. Use the outside end to work the heel. You can now use every inch of yarn that is left on the cuff.

19. Work the heel just like the toe, except in reverse. Join the yarn at one side of heel opening. Work single crochets around the heel opening. Place markers on each end so there are the same number of stitches on each side. Decrease before and after each marker until the stitch count is the same as the stitch count on round 1 of the toe. Turn sock inside out and whipstitch heel closed.

20. To prevent holes on each end of the heel opening, single crochet decrease in each end while working the first round of single crochets. If there are holes after working the heel, use the ends and a tapestry needle to make a couple stitches to close the holes.

21. Crochet does not stretch the same as knitting. It is also less resilient. Your sock should be a little snug. If it is too long, the heel will bunch up. The cuff will also sag if it is too loose. On the other hand, if the sock is too tight, you will have difficulty pulling it over the heel when you put it on.

22. The amount of yarn in a skein or ball is call its "put-up." The put-up for sock yarn is generally enough to knit one or two socks. Crochet uses 30 percent more yarn. If you want a longer cuff, buy extra yarn.

23. Toes and heels are the first places to wear out. For more durable socks, try working the toe and heel with two strands of yarn. The toe and after-thought heel are worked exactly the same but in opposite directions—one with increases, the other with decreases.

24. For a hole in the heel, just frog it and add a new heel. If there is a hole in the toe, pick the stitches out until there is an even round. Work a round of single crochets through the bottom of each stitch. Work a top-down toe just like the heel.

FIBER CONTENT

The fiber content tells what the yarn is. Wool fibers have scales. They look like the damaged hair shown in shampoo advertisements. When wool is exposed to moisture, variable temperatures and agitation, those scales hook into each other like Velcro® and cause the fabric to shrink and felt. Untreated wool should be hand-washed, rinsed in cool water and allowed to air dry.

But, who wants to hand-wash socks? If you like wool but not hand-washing, try a superwash.

Superwash wool is chemically treated to remove or coat the scales and prevent felting and shrinking. It is also less itchy. Many of the sock yarns available have some elastic or nylon in them to improve the durability. If you put the effort into socks, you want them to last.

Acrylic yarn has come a long way in the last 10 to 20 years. However, it still is not the best fiber to use for socks to wear inside shoes or to do much walking.

Microfiber is another form of acrylic and does not wear well for socks. These fibers are inexpensive, easily washable and come in a great variety of colors and textures, but are best used for slippers or bed socks that do not have to withstand everyday use.

SELF-STRIPING YARN

Self-striping sock yarn is designed for knitting in stockinette stitch. Because crochet uses 30 percent more yarn, the stripes will come out differently than in knit socks. Knitting uses one basic stitch made in two directions. There are varieties of crochet stitches worked in countless combinations. These different stitches also use varying amounts of yarn and therefore affect the striping pattern. A slight variation in tension or stitch count will also affect the stripes. So, do not worry about getting the stripes or the color sequence the same on both socks. It is nice when they do match, but do not drive yourself crazy.

DECREASING

Many decreases are made by working single crochet decrease or by skipping a stitch. This leaves a hole.

BLIND DECREASE

Insert the hook into the front loop of each of the next 2 stitches and pull up a loop through both stitches at once. Then, finish the single crochet. Bravo—less of a hole.

FOUNDATION SINGLE CROCHET

Ch 2, insert hook in 2nd ch from hook, pull lp through, yo, pull through 1 lp on hook (ch 1 completed), yo, pull through all lps on hook (sc completed).

Here is the tricky part. Insert the hook into the ch-1 stitch between the lps and under the back bar. Pull up a lp and make a ch. Yo, then finish the sc.

To make the heel opening, skip the ch-2 at the beginning. Insert your hook in the same stitch as the last stitch made, pull up a lp and make the ch, then finish the sc. ■

Denim Blue

SKILL LEVEL

INTERMEDIATE

FINISHED SIZES

Women's sock size given for 7–9 (small); changes for 9–11 (medium) and 10–12 (large) are in [ ].

MATERIALS

- Premier Serenity super fine (sock) weight yarn (1¾ oz/230 yds/50g per ball): SUPER FINE
  2 [2, 3] balls #DN104-06 indigo
- Size 4/2.00mm steel crochet hook or size needed to obtain gauge
- Tapestry needle
- Stitch marker

GAUGE

27 sc = 4 inches; 34 sc rows = 4 inches

Take time to check gauge.

PATTERN NOTES

Work in continuous rounds, do not turn or join unless otherwise stated.

Mark first stitch of each round.

Join with slip stitch as indicated unless otherwise stated.

INSTRUCTIONS
SOCK
MAKE 2.
CUFF RIBBING

Row 1 (RS): Ch 46 [41, 51], sc in 2nd ch from hook (*first sc does not count as first st*), [insert hook in same ch as last st, yo, pull up lp, insert hook in next ch, yo, pull lp through ch and all lps on hook] across, sl st in same ch last worked in (*sl st counts as last st*), turn.

Row 2: Ch 1, working in **back lps** (*see Stitch Guide*), sc in sl st, [insert hook in same st as last sc, yo, pull lp through, insert hook in next st, yo, pull lp through st and all lps on hook] across, leaving beg sc unworked, sl st in same st as last st worked, turn.

Next rows: Rep row 2 until piece measures 7 [7½, 8½] inches from beg. At end of last row, fasten off.

TOE

Rnd 1: Ch 15, sc in 2nd ch from hook and in each ch across to last ch, 3 sc in last ch, place marker in center sc in last ch, working on opposite side of ch, sc in each ch across to last ch, 2 sc in last ch, **do not join** (*see Pattern Notes*). (30 sc)

Rnd 2: [2 sc in next st, sc in each sc across to 1 st before marker, 2 sc in next st, sc in marked st, move marker] around.

Next rnds: Rep row 2 until there are 48 [54, 62] sts.

FOOT
Next rnds: Work even until Sock measures 7 [9½, 10] inches from beg.

HEEL OPENING
Next rnd: Fold Toe flat, sc across to next fold, ch 26 [29, 33], sk next 24 [27, 31] sts.

Next rnd: Sc in each st and in each ch around.

Next rnds: Work even until piece measures 1¼ inches from beg of Heel. At end of last rnd, fasten off.

HEEL
Rnd 1: Join (see Pattern Notes) at 1 end of Heel Opening, place marker, evenly sp 50 [56, 64] sc around opening, place marker at each side of Heel Opening so there are 24 [27, 31] sc between each marker.

Rnd 2: [Sc in each st around to 2 sts before marker, **sc dec** (see Stitch Guide) in next 2 sts, sc in marked st, move marker, sc dec in next 2 sts] around.

Next rnds: Rep rnd 2 until there are 30 sts. At end of last rnd, leaving long end, fasten off.

Turn Sock WS out, using long end, sew opening on Heel closed.

Turn RS out.

FINISHING
Sl st short ends of Ribbing tog to form tube.

With RS facing, sew Cuff to top of Foot. ∎

River Moss

SKILL LEVEL
INTERMEDIATE

FINISHED SIZES
Women's sock size given for 7–9 (small); changes for 9–11 (medium) and 10–12 (large) are in [ ].

MATERIALS
- Cascade Fixation light (DK) weight yarn (1¾ oz/100 yds/50g per ball): 2 [2, 3] balls #9939 green variegated 1 [1, 1] ball #8797 gray
- Size 4/2.00mm steel crochet hook or size needed to obtain gauge
- Tapestry needle
- Stitch marker

GAUGE
27 sc = 4 inches; 34 sc rows = 4 inches

Take time to check gauge.

PATTERN NOTES

Work in continuous rounds, do not turn or join unless otherwise stated.

Mark first stitch of each round.

Join with slip stitch as indicated unless otherwise stated.

Chain-2 at beginning of round counts as first double crochet unless otherwise stated.

INSTRUCTIONS
SOCK
MAKE 2.
TOE

Rnd 1: With gray, ch 15, sc in 2nd ch from hook and in each ch across to last ch, 3 sc in last ch, place marker in center sc of sc group, working on opposite side of ch, sc in each ch across with 2 sc in last ch, place marker in last st, **do not join** *(see Pattern Notes). (30 sc)*

Rnd 2: [2 sc in next st, sc in each st across to 1 st before next marker, 2 sc in next st, sc in marked st, move marker] around.

Next rnds: Rep rnd 2 until there are 48 [54, 62] sc.

Next rnd: 2 sc in first st, sc in each rem st around. *(49 [55, 63] sc)*

Next rnds: Work even until piece measures 2 inches from beg. At end of last rnd, **join** *(see Pattern Notes)* in beg sc. Fasten off.

INSTEP

Rnd 1: Join green variegated with sc in first st on Toe, [dc in next st, sc in next st] around, do not join.

Rnd 2: Dc in each sc and sc in each dc around.

Next rnds: Rep rnd 2 until piece measures 7 [8½, 10] inches from beg.

HEEL OPENING

Fold Toe flat, work in pattern to fold, ch 25 [29, 33], sk next 23 [27, 31] sts, sc in next dc.

ANKLE

Rnd 1: Work in established pattern in each st and in each ch around.

Next rnds: Continue in pattern until piece measures 13 [13, 15] inches from beg. At end of last rnd, fasten off.

RIBBING

Rnd 1: Join gray in center back of Sock, **ch 2** *(see Pattern Notes)*, dc in each st around, join in 2nd ch of beg ch-2.

Rnd 2: Ch 2, [**fpdc** *(see Stitch Guide)* around next st, **bpdc** *(see Stitch Guide)* around next st] around, join in 2nd ch of beg ch-2.

Next rnds: Rep rnd 2 until Ribbing measures 2 inches from beg. At end of last rnd, fasten off.

HEEL

Rnd 1: Join gray at 1 end of Heel Opening, place marker, evenly sp 50 [56, 64] sc around opening, place marker at each side of opening so there are 24 [27, 31] sts between markers.

Rnd 2: [Sc in each sc around to 2 sts before next marker, **sc dec** *(see Stitch Guide)*, sc in marked st, move marker, sc dec in next 2 sts] around.

Next rnds: Rep rnd 2 until there are 30 sts. At end of last rnd, leaving long end, fasten off.

Turn Sock inside out and with long end, sew opening closed.

Turn right side out. ∎

Rose Quartz

SKILL LEVEL

INTERMEDIATE

FINISHED SIZES

Women's sock size given for 7–9 (*small*); changes for 9–11 (*medium*) and 10–12 (*large*) are in [ ].

MATERIALS

- Premier Serenity super fine (sock) weight yarn (1¾ oz/230 yds/50g per ball):
  2 [2, 3] balls #DN104-04 purple spice
- Size 4/2.00mm steel crochet hook or size needed to obtain gauge
- Tapestry needle
- Stitch marker

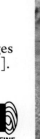

1 SUPER FINE

GAUGE

27 sc = 4 inches; 34 sc rows = 4 inches

Take time to check gauge.

PATTERN NOTES

Work in continuous rounds, do not turn or join unless otherwise stated.

Mark first stitch of each round.

Join with slip stitch as indicated unless otherwise stated.

INSTRUCTIONS
SOCK
MAKE 2.
TOE

Rnd 1: Ch 15, sc in 2nd ch from hook and in each ch across to last ch, 3 sc in last ch, place marker in center sc of sc group, working on opposite side of ch, sc in each ch across with 2 sc in last ch, place marker in last st, **do not join** (*see Pattern Notes*). (30 sc)

Rnd 2: [2 sc in next st, sc in each st across to 1 st before next marker, 2 sc in next st, sc in marked st, move marker] around.

Next rnds: Rep rnd 2 until there are 46 [54, 62] sc.

Next rnds: Work even until piece measures 2 inches from beg. At end of last rnd, **join** (*see Pattern Notes*) in beg sc.

INSTEP

Rnd 1: *Sk next st, 3 dc in next st**, sk next st, sc in next st, rep from * around, ending last rep at **. (12 [14, 16] dc groups)

Rnd 2: Sc in center dc of each dc group and 3 dc in each sc around.

Next rnds: Rep rnd 2 until piece measures 7 [8½, 10] inches from beg. At end of last rnd, join in beg sc. Fasten off.

HEEL OPENING

Fold Toe flat, in sc at fold, ch 26 [29, 33] sk next 24 [27, 31] sts, sl st next sc.

ANKLE

Rnd 1: Working in sts and chs, rep rnd 2 of Instep.

Next rnds: Rep rnd 2 of Instep until piece measures 14 [14, 15] inches from beg. At end of last rnd, join in beg sc.

CUFF

With WS facing, *ch 2, 5 dc in center dc of next dc group, ch 2**, sc in next sc, rep from * around, ending last rep at **, join in joining sl st of last rnd. Fasten off.

HEEL

Rnd 1: Join at 1 end of Heel Opening, place marker, evenly sp 50 [56, 64] sc around opening, place marker at each side of opening so there are 24 [27, 31] sts between markers.

Rnd 2: [Sc in each sc around to 2 sts before next marker, **sc dec** (see Stitch Guide), sc in marked st, move marker, sc dec in next 2 sts] around.

Next rnds: Rep rnd 2 until there are 30 sts. At end of last rnd, leaving long end, fasten off.

Turn Sock inside out and with long end, sew opening closed.

Turn right side out. ∎

Ocean Mist

SKILL LEVEL

INTERMEDIATE

FINISHED SIZES

Women's sock size given for 7–9 (small); changes for 9–11 (medium) and 10–12 (large) are in [ ].

MATERIALS

- Premier Serenity super fine (sock) weight yarn (1¾ oz/230 yds/50g per ball):
    2 [2, 3] balls #DN108-01 lavender topaz
- Size 4/2.00mm steel crochet hook or size needed to obtain gauge
- Tapestry needle
- Stitch marker

1 SUPER FINE

GAUGE

27 sc = 4 inches; 34 sc rows = 4 inches

Take time to check gauge.

PATTERN NOTES

Work in continuous rounds, do not turn or join unless otherwise stated.

Mark first stitch of each round.

Join with slip stitch as indicated unless otherwise stated.

Chain-3 at beginning of row or round counts as first double crochet unless otherwise stated.

SPECIAL STITCH

Cross stitch (cross-st): Sk next st, dc in next st, dc in st just sk.

INSTRUCTIONS
SOCK
MAKE 2.
TOE

Rnd 1: Ch 15, sc in 2nd ch from hook and in each ch across to last ch, 3 sc in last ch, place marker in center sc of sc group, working on opposite side of ch, sc in each ch across with 2 sc in last ch, place marker in last st, **do not join** *(see Pattern Notes)*. *(30 sc)*

Rnd 2: [2 sc in next st, sc in each st across to 1 st before next marker, 2 sc in next st, sc in marked st, move marker] around.

Next rnds: Rep rnd 2 until there are 48 [54, 62] sc.

Next rnds: Work even until piece measures 2 inches from beg. At end of last rnd, **join** *(see Pattern Notes)* in beg sc.

INSTEP

Rnd 1: Ch 3 *(see Pattern Notes)*, dc in previous st, **cross-st** *(see Special Stitch)* around, join in 3rd ch of beg ch-3.

Next rnds: Rep rnd 1 until piece measures 7 [8½, 10] inches from beg. At end of last rnd, fasten off.

HEEL OPENING

Fold Toe flat, join at next fold in 2nd st of cross-st, ch 26 [29, 33] sk next 24 [27, 31] sts, sl st in each of next 2 sts.

ANKLE

Next rnd: Rep rnd 1 of Instep, working in each st and in each ch around.

Next rnds: Rep rnd 1 of Instep until piece measures 14 [13, 15] inches from beg. At end of last rnd, fasten off.

RIBBING

Row 1: Ch 8, sc in **back bar** *(see illustration)* of 2nd ch from hook and in back bar of each ch across, turn. *(7 sc)*

Back Bar of Chain

Row 2: Working in **back lps** *(see Stitch Guide)*, ch 1, sc in each st across, turn.

Next rows: Rep row 2 until piece measures 7 [8½, 9] inches from beg. At end of last row, fasten off.

FINISHING

Sew short ends of Ribbing tog, forming a tube.

Sew 1 end of tube to last rnd of Ankle.

HEEL

Rnd 1: Join at 1 end of Heel Opening, place marker, evenly sp 50 [56, 64] sc around opening, place marker at each side of opening so there are 24 [27, 31] sts between markers.

Rnd 2: [Sc in each sc around to 2 sts before next marker, **sc dec** *(see Stitch Guide)*, sc in marked st, move marker, sc dec in next 2 sts] around.

Next rnds: Rep rnd 2 until there are 30 sts. At end of last rnd, leaving long end, fasten off.

Turn Sock inside out and with long end, sew opening closed.

Turn RS out. ■

Painted Desert

SKILL LEVEL

INTERMEDIATE

FINISHED SIZES
Women's sock size given for 7–9 *(small);* changes
for 9–11 *(medium)* and 10–12 *(large)* are in [ ].

MATERIALS
- Premier Serenity super fine (sock)
  weight yarn (1¾ oz/230 yds/50g
  per ball):
  2 [2, 3] balls DN108-07 citrine
- Size 4/2.00mm steel crochet hook
  or size needed to obtain gauge
- Tapestry needle
- Stitch marker

1 SUPER FINE

GAUGE
27 sc = 4 inches; 34 sc rows = 4 inches

Take time to check gauge.

PATTERN NOTES
Work in continuous rounds, do not turn or join
unless otherwise stated.

Mark first stitch of each round.

Join with slip stitch as indicated unless
otherwise stated.

Chain-3 at beginning of row or round counts as
first double crochet unless otherwise stated.

SPECIAL STITCH
Cluster (cl): Holding back last lp of each st on
hook, 5 dc in place indicated, yo, pull through
all lps on hook, ch 1 to close.

INSTRUCTIONS
SOCK
MAKE 2.
TOE
Rnd 1: Ch 15, sc in 2nd ch from hook and in
each ch across to last ch, 3 sc in last ch, place

marker in center sc of sc group, working on
opposite side of ch, sc in each ch across with
2 sc in last ch, place marker in last st, **do not
join** *(see Pattern Notes). (30 sc)*

Rnd 2: [2 sc in next st, sc in each st across to 1 st
before next marker, 2 sc in next st, sc in marked
st, move marker] around.

Next rnds: Rep rnd 2 until there are 48
[54, 62] sc.

Next rnds: Work even until piece measures
2 inches from beg. At end of last rnd, **join**
(see Pattern Notes) in beg sc.

FOOT
Next rnds: Work even until piece measures
7 [8½, 10] inches from beg.

HEEL OPENING

Fold Toe Flat, sc to next fold, ch 26 [29, 33], sk next 24 [27, 31] sts, sc in next st.

ANKLE

Rnd 1: Working in sts and in chs, **ch 3** (see Pattern Notes), dc in next st, [**cl** (see Special Stitch) in next st, dc in each of next 5 sts] around, ending with dc in each of last 0 [0, 2] st(s), join in 3rd ch of beg ch-3, turn.

Next rnds: Rep rnd 1 until Ankle measures 3 [3, 5] inches from beg, ending on WS rnd.

Last rnd. Ch 3, dc in each st around, join in 3rd ch of beg ch-3, **do not turn.**

RIBBING

Rnd 1: Ch 2 (counts as first dc on Ribbing rnds), [**fpdc** (see Stitch Guide) around next st, **bpdc** (see Stitch Guide) around next st] around, join in 2nd ch of beg ch-2.

Next rnds: Rep rnd 1 until Ribbing is 1½ [1½, 2] inches from beg. At end of last rnd, fasten off.

HEEL

Rnd 1: Join at 1 end of Heel Opening, place marker, evenly sp 50 [56, 64] sc around opening, place marker at each side of opening so there are 24 [27, 31] sts between markers.

Rnd 2: [Sc in each sc around to 2 sts before next marker, **sc dec** (see Stitch Guide) in next 2 sts, sc in marked st, move marker, sc dec in next 2 sts] around.

Next rnds: Rep rnd 2 until there are 30 sts. At end of last rnd, leaving long end, fasten off.

Turn Sock inside out and with long end, sew opening closed.

Turn right side out. ■

Rugged Entrelac

SKILL LEVEL

INTERMEDIATE

FINISHED SIZES

Instructions given for man's shoe size 6–8 (small); changes for 8½–10 (medium) and 10½–12 (large) are in [ ].

MATERIALS

- Cascade Fixation light (DK) weight yarn (1¾ oz/100 yds/50g per ball): 2 [2, 3] balls each #7988 brown and #9886 variegated
- Size 4/2.00mm steel crochet hook or size needed to obtain gauge
- Tapestry needle
- Stitch marker

GAUGE

27 sc = 4 inches; 34 sc rows = 4 inches

Take time to check gauge.

PATTERN NOTES

Work in continuous rounds; do not turn or join unless otherwise stated.

Mark first stitch of each round.

Join with slip stitch as indicated unless otherwise stated.

Chain-2 at beginning of row or round counts as first double crochet unless otherwise stated.

INSTRUCTIONS
SOCK
MAKE 2.
TOE

Rnd 1: With brown, ch 15, sc in 2nd ch from hook and in each ch across to last ch, 3 sc in last ch, place marker in center sc of sc group, working on opposite side of ch, sc in each ch across with 2 sc in last ch, place marker in last st, **do not join** *(see Pattern Notes). (30 sc)*

Rnd 2: [2 sc in next st, sc in each st across to 1 st before next marker, 2 sc in next st, sc in marked st, move marker] around.

Next rnds: Rep rnd 2 until there are 48 [54, 62] sc.

Next rnd: 2 sc in first st, sc in each rem st around. *(49 [55, 63] sc)*

Next rnds: Work even until piece measures 2 inches from beg. At end of last rnd, **join** *(see Pattern Notes)* in beg sc. Fasten off.

FOOT

Next rnds: Join variegated with sc in first st, work even until piece measures 7½ [8½, 9] inches from beg.

HEEL OPENING

Next rnd: Fold Toe flat, sc to next fold, ch 26 [29, 33], sk next 24 [27, 31] sts, sc in next st.

Next rnd: Sc in each st and in each ch around and **at the same time,** evenly sp (2 sc in next st) 4 [7, 8] times. *(55 [64, 73] sc)*

Next rnd: Sc in each st around.

ANKLE

Rnd 1: Sc in next st, insert hook under 2nd leg of sc just worked, yo, pull lp through, insert hook in next sc, yo, pull up lp *(3 lps on hook)*, [yo, pull through 2 lps on hook] twice, work the following steps to complete this rnd:

A. Pull up lp in each of 2nd and 3rd vertical bars, pull up lp in next sc *(4 lps on hook)*, [yo, pull through 2 lps on hook] across;

B. Sk first vertical bar, pull up lp in each of next 3 vertical bars, pull up lp in next sc *(5 lps on hook)*, [yo, pull through 2 lps on hook] across;

C. Sk first vertical bar, pull up lp in each of next 4 vertical bars, pull up lp in next sc *(6 lps on hook)*, [yo, pull through 2 lps on hook] across;

D. Sk first vertical bar, pull up lp in each of next 5 vertical bars, pull up lp in next sc *(7 lps on hook)*, [yo, pull through 2 lps on hook] across;

E. Sk first vertical bar, pull up lp in each of next 6 vertical bars, pull up lp in next sc *(8 lps on hook)*, [yo, pull through 2 lps on hook] across;

F. Sk first vertical bar, pull up lp in each of next 7 vertical bars, pull up lp in next sc *(9 lps on hook)*, [yo, pull through 2 lps on hook] across;

G. Sk first vertical bar, pull up lp in each of next 8 vertical bars, pull up lp in next sc *(10 lps on hook)*, [yo, pull through 2 lps on hook] across;

H. Sl st in each of next 9 vertical bars *(triangle completed)*;

I. Sc in next st, insert hook under 2nd leg of sc just worked, yo, pull lp through, insert hook in next sc, yo, pull up lp, *(3 lps on hook)*, [yo, pull through 2 lps on hook] twice;

J. [Rep steps A–I] around, ending last rep with step H. At end of last step, sl st in last st. Fasten off.

Rnd 2: Join variegated in point of next triangle, pull up lp in each of next 7 sl sts, sk last sl st, pull up lp in end of first row of next triangle *(9 lps on hook)*, [yo, pull through 2 lps on hook] across, work the following steps to complete this rnd:

A. Pull up lp in each of next 7 vertical bars, pull up lp in end of row on next triangle (*9 lps on hook*), [yo, pull through 2 lps on hook] across;

B. Rep step A 7 times;

C. Sl st in each of next 8 vertical bars, sl st in next triangle;

D. Pull up lp in each of next 7 sl sts, sk last sl st, pull up lp in end of first row of next triangle (*9 lps on hook*), [yo, pull through 2 lps on hook] across (*square completed*);

E. Rep steps A–D around, ending last rep with step C;

F. Fasten off.

Rnds 3–8: Join next color in point of next square, rep rnd 2.

Rnd 9: Join brown in point of next square, pull up lp in each of next 6 sl sts, pull up lp in end of row on next square (*8 lps on hook*), [yo, pull through 2 lps on hook] 5 times, yo, pull through last 3 lps on hook, work the following steps to complete this rnd:

A. Sk next vertical bar, pull up lp in each of next 5 vertical bars, pull up lp in end of next row on square (*7 lps on hook*), [yo, pull through 2 lps on hook] 4 times, yo, pull through last 3 lps on hook;

B. Sk next vertical bar, pull up lp in each of next 4 vertical bars, pull up lp in end of next row on square (*6 lps on hook*), [yo, pull through 2 lps on hook] 3 times, yo, pull through last 3 lps on hook;

C. Sk next vertical bar, pull up lp in each of next 3 vertical bars, pull up lp in end of next row on square (*5 lps on hook*), [yo, pull through 2 lps on hook] twice, yo, pull through last 3 lps on hook;

D. Sk next vertical bar, pull up lp in each of next 2 vertical bars, pull up lp in end of next row on square (*4 lps on hook*), yo, pull through 2 lps on hook, yo, pull through last 3 lps on hook;

E. Sk next vertical bar, pull up lp in next vertical bar, pull up lp in end of next row on square (*3 lps on hook*), yo, pull through 3 lps on hook;

F. Sl st in end of next row and first sl st of next square;

G. Pull up lp in each of next 6 sl sts, pull up lp in end of row on next square (*8 lps on hook*), [yo, pull through 2 lps on hook] 5 times, yo, pull through last 3 lps on hook,

H. Rep steps A–G around, ending last rep at end of step F.

I. Fasten off.

RIBBING
Rnd 1: Join brown in center back of Sock, **ch 2** (*see Pattern Notes*), dc in each st around, join in 2nd ch of beg ch-2.

Rnd 2: Ch 2, [**fpdc** (*see Stitch Guide*) around next st, **bpdc** (*see Stitch Guide*) around next st] around, join in 2nd ch of beg ch-2.

Next rnds: Rep rnd 2 until Ribbing measures 1½ inches from beg. At end of last row, fasten off.

HEEL
Rnd 1: Join brown with sc at 1 end of Heel Opening, place marker, evenly sp 50 [56, 64] sc around opening, place marker at each side of opening so there are 24 [27, 31] sts between markers.

Rnd 2: [Sc in each sc around to 2 sts before next marker, **sc dec** (*see Stitch Guide*) in next 2 sts, sc in marked st, move marker, sc dec in next 2 sts] around.

Next rnds: Rep rnd 2 until there are 30 sts. At end of last rnd, leaving long end, fasten off.

Turn Sock inside out and with long end, sew opening closed.

Turn right side out. ∎

STITCH GUIDE

STITCH ABBREVIATIONS

beg . . . . begin/begins/beginning
bpdc . . . . back post double crochet
bpsc . . . . back post single crochet
bptr . . . . back post treble crochet
CC . . . . contrasting color
ch(s) . . . . chain(s)
ch- . . . . refers to chain or space
previously made (i.e., ch-1 space)
ch sp(s) . . . . chain space(s)
cl(s) . . . . cluster(s)
cm . . . . centimeter(s)
dc . . . . double crochet (singular/plural)
dc dec . . . . double crochet 2 or more
stitches together, as indicated
dec. . . . . decrease/decreases/decreasing
dtr . . . . double treble crochet
ext . . . . extended
fpdc . . . . front post double crochet
fpsc . . . . front post single crochet
fptr . . . . front post treble crochet
g . . . . gram(s)
hdc . . . . half double crochet
hdc dec . . . . half double crochet 2 or more
stitches together, as indicated
inc . . . . increase/increases/increasing
lp(s) . . . . loop(s)
MC . . . . main color
mm . . . . millimeter(s)
oz . . . . ounce(s)
pc . . . . popcorn(s)
rem . . . . remain/remains/remaining
rep(s) . . . . repeat(s)
rnd(s) . . . . round(s)
RS . . . . right side
sc . . . . single crochet (singular/plural)
sc dec . . . . single crochet 2 or more
stitches together, as indicated
sk . . . . skip/skipped/skipping
sl st(s) . . . . slip stitch(es)
sp(s) . . . . space(s)/spaced
st(s) . . . . stitch(es)
tog . . . . together
tr . . . . treble crochet
trtr . . . . .triple treble
WS . . . . wrong side
yd(s) . . . . yard(s)
yo . . . . yarn over

YARN CONVERSION

OUNCES TO GRAMS		GRAMS TO OUNCES	
1	28.4	25	⅞
2	56.7	40	1⅔
3	85.0	50	1¾
4	113.4	100	3½

UNITED STATES		UNITED KINGDOM
sl st (slip stitch)	=	sc (single crochet)
sc (single crochet)	=	dc (double crochet)
hdc (half double crochet)	=	htr (half treble crochet)
dc (double crochet)	=	tr (treble crochet)
tr (treble crochet)	=	dtr (double treble crochet)
dtr (double treble crochet)	=	ttr (triple treble crochet)
skip	=	miss

Single crochet decrease (sc dec): (Insert hook, yo, draw lp through) in each of the sts indicated, yo, draw through all lps on hook.

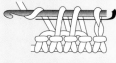

Example of 2-sc dec

Half double crochet decrease (hdc dec): (Yo, insert hook, yo, draw lp through) in each of the sts indicated, yo, draw through all lps on hook.

Example of 2-hdc dec

Reverse Single Crochet (reverse sc): Ch 1. Skip first st. [Working from left to right, insert hook in next st from front to back, draw up lp on hook, yo, and draw through both lps on hook.]

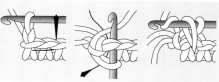

Chain (ch): Yo, pull through lp on hook.

Single crochet (sc): Insert hook in st, yo, pull through st, yo, pull through both lps on hook.

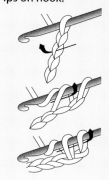

Double crochet (dc): Yo, insert hook in st, yo, pull through st, [yo, pull through 2 lps] twice.

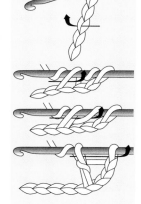

Double crochet decrease (dc dec): Yo, insert hook, yo, draw loop through, draw through 2 lps on hook) in each of the sts indicated, yo, draw through all lps on hook.

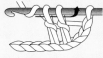

Example of 2-dc dec

Front loop (front lp) Back loop (back lp)

Front Loop   Back Loop

Front post stitch (fp): Back post stitch (bp): When working post st, insert hook from right to left around post st on previous row.

Back   Front

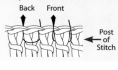

← Post of Stitch

Half double crochet (hdc): Yo, insert hook in st, yo, pull through st, yo, pull through all 3 lps on hook.

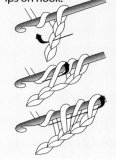

Double treble crochet (dtr): Yo 3 times, insert hook in st, yo, pull through st, [yo, pull through 2 lps] 4 times.

Treble crochet decrease (tr dec): Holding back last lp of each st, tr in each of the sts indicated, yo, pull through all lps on hook.

Example of 2-tr dec

Slip stitch (sl st): Insert hook in st, pull through both lps on hook.

Chain Color Change (ch color change) Yo with new color, draw through last lp on hook.

Double Crochet Color Change (dc color change) Drop first color, yo with new color, draw through last 2 lps of st.

Treble crochet (tr): Yo twice, insert hook in st, yo, pull through st, [yo, pull through 2 lps] 3 times.

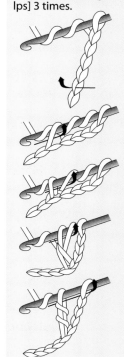

Metric Conversion Charts

METRIC CONVERSIONS				
yards	x	.9144	=	metres (m)
yards	x	91.44	=	centimetres (cm)
inches	x	2.54	=	centimetres (cm)
inches	x	25.40	=	millimetres (mm)
inches	x	.0254	=	metres (m)

centimetres	x	.3937	=	inches
metres	x	1.0936	=	yards

INCHES INTO MILLIMETRES & CENTIMETRES (Rounded off slightly)

inches	mm	cm	inches	cm	inches	cm	inches	cm
1/8	3	0.3	5	12.5	21	53.5	38	96.5
1/4	6	0.6	5 1/2	14	22	56	39	99
3/8	10	1	6	15	23	58.5	40	101.5
1/2	13	1.3	7	18	24	61	41	104
5/8	15	1.5	8	20.5	25	63.5	42	106.5
3/4	20	2	9	23	26	66	43	109
7/8	22	2.2	10	25.5	27	68.5	44	112
1	25	2.5	11	28	28	71	45	114.5
1 1/4	32	3.2	12	30.5	29	73.5	46	117
1 1/2	38	3.8	13	33	30	76	47	119.5
1 3/4	45	4.5	14	35.5	31	79	48	122
2	50	5	15	38	32	81.5	49	124.5
2 1/2	65	6.5	16	40.5	33	84	50	127
3	75	7.5	17	43	34	86.5		
3 1/2	90	9	18	46	35	89		
4	100	10	19	48.5	36	91.5		
4 1/2	115	11.5	20	51	37	94		

KNITTING NEEDLES CONVERSION CHART

Canada/U.S.	0	1	2	3	4	5	6	7	8	9	10	10½	11	13	15
Metric (mm)	2	2¼	2¾	3¼	3½	3¾	4	4½	5	5½	6	6½	8	9	10

CROCHET HOOKS CONVERSION CHART

Canada/U.S.	1/B	2/C	3/D	4/E	5/F	6/G	8/H	9/I	10/J	10½/K	N
Metric (mm)	2.25	2.75	3.25	3.5	3.75	4.25	5	5.5	6	6.5	9.0

Annie's Attic®

RETAIL STORES: If you would like to carry this pattern book or any other DRG publications, visit DRGwholesale.com.

Every effort has been made to ensure that the instructions in this publication are complete and accurate. We cannot, however, take responsibility for human error, typographical mistakes or variations in individual work. Please visit AnniesCustomerCare.com to check for pattern updates.

ISBN: 978-1-59635-317-6

2 3 4 5 6 7 8 9